A fisherman drinks in the twilight as he drifts peacefully on Yellowstone Lake.   MICHAEL SAMPLE

" *In Yellowstone, the resource is not twenty thousand elk, or a million lodgepole pines, or a grizzly bear. The resource is* wildness. *The interplay of all the parts of the wilderness—weather, animals, plants, earthquakes—acting upon each other to create the wild setting, creates a state of existence, a wildness, that is the product and the resource for which Yellowstone is being preserved.* "

Don Despain
quoted in *Mountain Time*

Six-point bull elk plodding across a calm stretch of the Yellowstone River.
MICHAEL SAMPLE

3

4

Bison graze in the rolling swales of the Hayden Valley. MICHAEL SAMPLE

Soda Butte Creek and its valley, a favorite bison hangout. JOHN REDDY

A wildflower garden near cascading Lewis Falls. GLENN VAN NIMWEGEN

" *If I could choose only one sight in the wonderland, it would be. . .that view from the top of Mount Washburn, for you see there the entire Park spread out before you in a single picture. . . the mighty Canon, holding the two falls of the Yellowstone. . . . Then the rich luxuriant growth of green pines, so vast & numberless that you can count them only as the blades of grass on the prairie. . . . And encircling all and towering above all as far as the eye can reach rise the massive chain of the Rocky Mountains covered on their summitts with eternal snow.* "

Colgate Hoyt, 1878
"Roughing it up the Yellowstone to Wonderland"

6

Two summer standbys: blue-pod lupine and
Indian paintbrush. MICHAEL SAMPLE

The view from Mount Washburn, reaching to the Grand Canyon of the Yellowstone and the distant Absaroka Mountains.
GEORGE WUERTHNER

Seasons after the park's massive burn, arrowleaf balsamroot blooms burst from the hills near Elk Creek. GEORGE WUERTHNER

Spring regeneration and a mosaic of burned trees on Antelope Creek. JEFF AND ALEXA HENRY

Fireweed and heartleaf arnica are among the first
wildflowers to reseed the blackened ground.
MICHAEL SAMPLE

66 *Lush and green, it was a quiet retreat
from the frenzied pace of summer. I would
miss it. I felt the sorrow of a friend lost. And
yet, looking closer, I saw that within a
month, vibrant, green grasses had begun
sprouting up everywhere. . . .The senescent
and dying lodgepole forest was springing to
life again.* 99

Carol A. Shively
"A Smoke-Scented Diary"

An aerial view of the Yellowstone River near Mud Volcano, capturing steam from the Dragon's Mouth. DENVER BRYAN

" *There are places in the park where the earth seems eerily alive, as boiling water beneath the ground causes it to tremble and the sultry stink of sulfur fills the air.*

The earth seems like it is straining to speak here. Or perhaps sing, a ghostly-sounding geyser choir—throaty roars, sputters, rumbles, hissing and deep gargles emanating from the holes in the ground. "

Jim Robbins
Last Refuge

Shell Geyser, in Biscuit Basin. MICHAEL SAMPLE

Minerals precipitate from the hot water to create the ring around this pool in the Upper Geyser Basin. MICHAEL SAMPLE

The multicolored channels of Grand Prismatic Spring, in Midway Geyser Basin.   JOHN REDDY

Visitors explore the Lower Geyser Basin on a protective boardwalk. BUDDY MAYS

" In no country on the globe, within the same area, has Nature crowded so much of grandeur and majesty, with so much of novelty and variety. Unlike any other scenery of the world, and unrivaled in wild and weird wonders, the Upper Yellowstone, the geysers, the mountains, lakes, and valleys, of this country will always draw the lovers of the marvelous in Nature."

Edwin J. Stanley
Rambles in Wonderland, 1878

Water vapor forms a signal from the ramparts of Castle Geyser. MICHAEL SAMPLE

Riverside Geyser spits and spurts near the Firehole River. MICHAEL SAMPLE

A volcanic black sand beach on Yellowstone Lake. MICHAEL SAMPLE

Thirsty bison seeking a cold drink from the azure lake. MICHAEL SAMPLE

Lake Hotel, one of the park's turn-of-the-century landmarks. CAROL POLICH

Canada geese frequent the glassy Yellowstone River where it flows through Hayden Valley. MICHAEL SAMPLE

> ❝ *Every artist of genius experiences during his life a great spiritual revelation and upheaval. This revelation came to Thomas Moran as he journeyed on horseback through an almost unbelievable wilderness. To him it was all grandeur, beauty, color, and light— nothing of man at all, but nature, virgin, unspoiled and lovely. In the Yellowstone country he found fairy-like color and form that his dreams could not rival.* ❞

The artist's daughter, recalling his inspirations

Trout Creek's silver loops and bends, at dawn.   MICHAEL SAMPLE

A wintering trumpeter swan, one of North America's largest birds.   JEFF FOOTT

Snow lingers in the shadowy canyon at Undine Falls. GLENN VAN NIMWEGEN

The crisp contrasts of winter in a reflective pond near the park's East Entrance. MICHAEL SAMPLE

66 Yellowstone during the short days of mid-December is like a place above the Arctic Circle. 99

Jim Robbins
Last Refuge

Transparent and glassy icicles form near many of the park's trickling springs. MICHAEL SAMPLE

Winter smoothes the shapely foothills above the Lamar River.   MICHAEL SAMPLE

On a sunny winter day, a coyote hunts and travels atop the snow's crust.
MICHAEL SAMPLE

Deep winter along Pebble Creek, a snowbound stream beneath Cutoff Mountain.   MICHAEL SAMPLE

One of the Gibbon River's many gurgling cascades.   MICHAEL SAMPLE

A multicolored hot spring mound along the Gibbon River. MICHAEL SAMPLE

A slender lodgepole pine projects its silhouette onto rocks in the Gibbon River canyon. MICHAEL SAMPLE

" At the head of this river the nativs give an account that there is frequently herd a loud noise, like Thunder, which makes the earth Tremble, they State that they seldom go there because their children Cannot sleep—and Conceive it possessed of spirits, who were averse that men Should be near them. "

William Clark
Lewis and Clark Expedition

Summer sunrise from the lush south flanks of Mount Washburn. MICHAEL SAMPLE

Moose mother and calf, making a lunch of tender spring growth. MICHAEL SAMPLE

Style met practical engineering at this old concrete bridge above the Upper Falls of the Yellowstone. CAROL POLICH

Sharply angled columnar basalt cuts through glacial till above the Yellowstone River.   MICHAEL SAMPLE

" Leaving the highway and walking through these vast, seemingly limitless swales of pine and grass provokes a kind of passionate serenity that I have known in few other places. It is a heartland without boundaries. "

Gary Ferguson
Walking Down the Wild

The remains of a Shoshoni or "Sheepeater" Indian wickiup at one of the park's many important archaeological sites.   MICHAEL SAMPLE

Dancing cottonwood in the Lamar Valley lives on despite its split trunk.   MICHAEL SAMPLE

Morning highlights in dewy foxtail grass west of Canyon Village.   MICHAEL SAMPLE

Lacy blooms of cow parsnip attract a dark-winged butterfly.   MICHAEL SAMPLE

A dewy thicket of cow parsnip beneath the volcanic Absaroka Mountains. GLENN VAN NIMWEGEN

Angling for Yellowstone cutthroat trout below LeHardys Rapids, on the Yellowstone River.   DENVER BRYAN

<blockquote>
“ A good fly-fisherman becomes a part of the river, like an otter or a heron, thinking about likely banks for a trout to hide under, worrying about the angle of approach so as not to be spotted, and causing the fly to behave in a natural way that entices the fish. Attention narrows down to the point where there is only the fish and the fisherman. ”
</blockquote>

Jim Robbins
Last Refuge

A trout's hovering pool.   MICHAEL SAMPLE

Enjoying the grand wildness of Antelope Creek valley. MICHAEL SAMPLE

Kicking back after a hike to Seven Mile Hole in the Grand Canyon of the Yellowstone. MICHAEL SAMPLE

66 *That much of the region is still untrammeled, there can be no doubt. As any backcountry junkie will tell you, there are plenty of places left where, but for the occasional jet trail leaking into the big sky, the land seems to have been somehow cast adrift from the moorings of the modern world. The seasons push and pull through the high country with the rhythm of thousands of years behind them.* 99

Gary Ferguson
Walking Down the Wild

Canoeing remote Shoshone Lake in September. GEORGE WUERTHNER

Casting through an ethereal fly hatch on the Yellowstone River. MICHAEL SAMPLE

A quartet of bulls at Cascade Creek. MICHAEL SAMPLE

This bull elk's antlers are still growing under their velvet covering. MICHAEL SAMPLE

" Yellowstone's very meaning. . .is nature: nature undefiled: a setting to awaken atavistic memories of the many-powered and mysterious world that filled the hearts of our ancestors with holy awe: the wild. We have set this land apart because we hallow it and the creatures who live here, and we hallow it and its creatures because they are wild. "

Thomas McNamee
The Grizzly Bear

Lilypads in limpid Isa Lake. JEFF FOOTT

Yellow pond lily. MICHAEL SAMPLE

A pothole pond ringed with the lush greenery of high summer.   ALAN A. CHAPMAN

Lilypads cover a glassy pond near the edge
of a burn.   MICHAEL SAMPLE

Sleek river otters stalk ducks along Elk Antler Creek.
MICHAEL SAMPLE

Fringed gentian. MICHAEL SAMPLE

A trio of arrowleaf balsamroot heads. MICHAEL SAMPLE

Giant red or Indian paintbrush. MICHAEL SAMPLE

Pasque flowers, some of the first blossoms to appear after snowmelt. MICHAEL SAMPLE

" Even in July and August both prairie and woodland bloom with flowers of brilliant hue, possessing all the freshness of spring. They seem to follow closely the melting snows up the highest mountainside, if possible to beautify and adorn Mother Earth with a gorgeous robe ere Winter comes again. . . "

Edwin J. Stanley
Rambles in Wonderland, 1878

Pearly everlasting and pink monkey flower near a cascade at the park's eastern edge. MICHAEL SAMPLE

> " *Nature has made her wildest patterns here, has brought the boiling waters from her greatest depths to the peaks which bear eternal snow, and set her masterpiece with pools like jewels. Let us respect her moods, and let the beasts she nurtures in her bosom live.* "

Frederic Remington
quoted in *Roadside History of Yellowstone Park*

The Hoodoos, limestone formations near Mammoth.
MICHAEL SAMPLE

A bull elk and his herd beneath the grand terrace at Mammoth Hot Springs.   JEFF FOOTT

Mammoth's Canary Spring. GLENN VAN NIMWEGEN

Elk are among the most frequent of visitors at the Albright Visitor Center in Mammoth. GLENN VAN NIMWEGEN

Stairstep pools at Minerva Terrace. MICHAEL SAMPLE

The site of old Fort Yellowstone, now the park community of Mammoth,
as seen from atop the hot springs mound. JOHN REDDY

*" To say that these rocky formations simulate cauliflower, sponge,
fleeces of wool, flowers or bead-work conveys but a feeble idea of
their marvelous beauty. "*

Hiram Martin Chittenden
The Yellowstone National Park, Historical and Descriptive

Full moon above the rim of a canyon near the park's north border. MICHAEL SAMPLE

Hotpotting where the Boiling River pours into the Gardner River's cooler flow.   JEFF AND ALEXA HENRY

" *I thanked God that right in the heart of all this noise & wrestless life*
of Millions a wise Government had forever set apart that marvelous
regeon as a National Park, where

     Mid the encircling snow clad mountains

     water falls & Canons grand,

     Bathing pools & spouting fountains

     Of that Mighty wonderland

the worn, the sick and jaded could ever find rest, and refreshment,
and opportunity to study the Master's *hand in nature.* "

Colgate Hoyt, 1878
including an excerpt from *The Calumet of the Coteau,*
quoted in *"Roughing it up the Yellowstone to Wonderland"*

Many visitors to Yellowstone pass through nearby Grand Teton National Park, where aspens glow beneath the Grand Tetons. FRED PFLUGHOFT

" *My heart's in the valleys
and parks of the West,
'Mid deer, elk, and
grizzly, of all game the best.
Farewell to my business,
farewell to my home;
Adieu to my loved ones,
my fate is to roam
'Mid the pure crystal
fountains and geysers below
The wild-circling
mountains, white-glistening
with snow.* "

Early Yellowstone National Park
superintendent P. W. Norris
The Calumet of the Coteau

Mule deer buck in sagebrush terrain. MICHAEL SAMPLE

Ephemeral falls on Barronette Peak. MICHAEL SAMPLE

Trumpeter swans stretch their long wings.   MICHAEL SAMPLE

A beaver pulling home an alder branch, part of the day's cut.   TOM MURPHY

A maze of bark and gray twigs on a burned flank of Mount Washburn. MICHAEL SAMPLE

National Park Service Ranger Naturalist Roy Wood interprets a burned area at the Children's Fire Trail.   JEFF AND ALEXA HENRY

Petrified Tree, a standing example of Yellowstone's vast fossilized forest.   MICHAEL SAMPLE

66 We are standing at a turning point in history, the birth of the new Yellowstone. Although the fire has created an artistic array of visual contrasts, beauty is in the eye of the beholder. Some will say "It's not pretty," and I wouldn't try to convince them otherwise. Birth never is. 99

Carol A. Shively
"A Smoke-Scented Diary"

53

Bighorn rams survey their realm. GLENN VAN NIMWEGEN

A flat-backed badger pauses in the midst of its digging.
MICHAEL SAMPLE

A weasel seems overexposed in its winter ermine coat,
when winter has not quite arrived. MICHAEL SAMPLE

Polished antler tines shine as a bull elk steps into one of the park's peaceful rivers. MICHAEL SAMPLE

The swift, sinuous shape of the Lewis River. MICHAEL SAMPLE

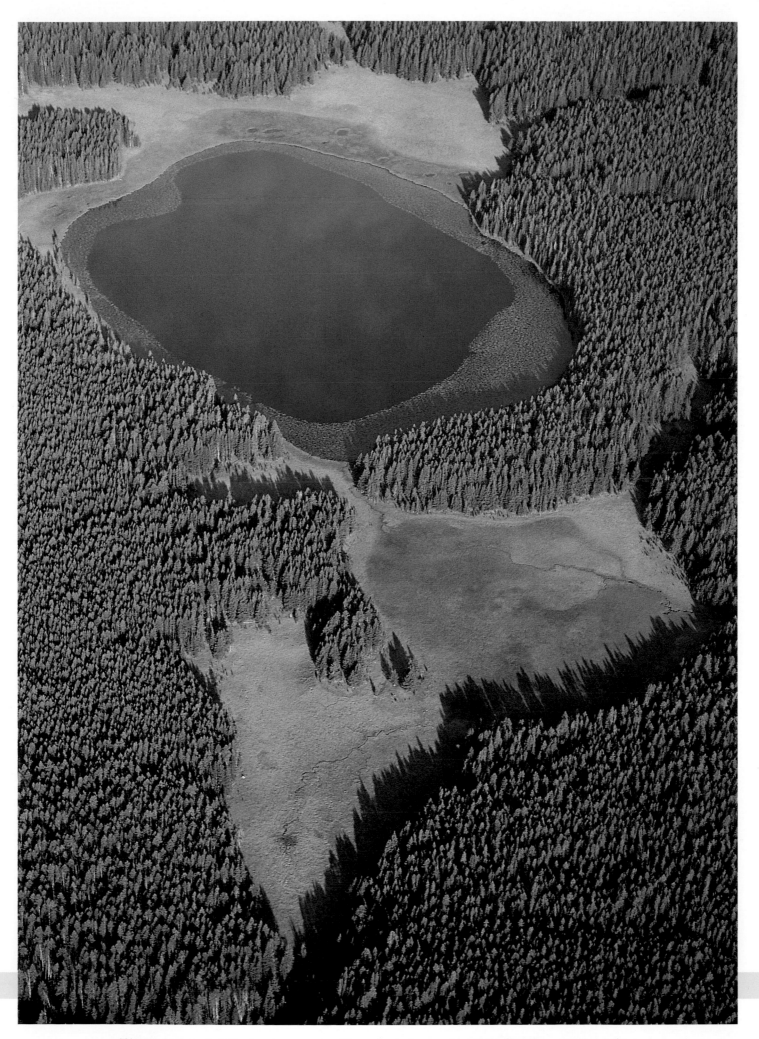

Woven textures of the landscape near Wrangler Lake, as seen from the sky.   MICHAEL SAMPLE

A trotting elk amid snowy ridges and billows.　CAROL POLICH

A jack rabbit sits still, confident of its winter camouflage.　MICHAEL SAMPLE

Massive ice builds up at the foot of the Lower Falls of the Yellowstone in winter.   CAROL POLICH

Looming from the fog, a bison seeks the wind shadow of a frosty pine. CAROL POLICH

Sawing snow blocks at Canyon Village to keep roofs from collapsing under winter's weight.   JEFF AND ALEXA HENRY

Lake Ranger Station as few see it.   JEFF AND ALEXA HENRY

❝ It's hard for most of us to even imagine what life is like for much of the year along these high, wild rooftops. Winter temperatures often plunge to thirty and forty below zero, and snow may accumulate to depths of twenty feet. The wind can blow a remarkably bitter tune. . .❞

Gary Ferguson
Walking Down the Wild

A rosy sunset on Elk Antler Creek.   MICHAEL SAMPLE

" *Small, precious [things] hint [at] the wild tapestry that once circled the earth,
the patterns and paradigms that first breathed meaning into human existence.
For many people those hints are what help transcend the tumult of daily living,
they are that slim measure of miracle that brings wholeness to a severed world.
Looking back, I realize that I too was hunting for such inklings, such assurances,
from the nooks and crannies of Yellowstone. And what is perhaps most
remarkable of all is that I never once failed to find them.* "

Gary Ferguson
Walking Down the Wild

White pelicans at dusk, below Fishing Bridge on the Yellowstone River. MICHAEL SAMPLE

Riding an old stagecoach to a cookout near Roosevelt Lodge.   ERWIN AND PEGGY BAUER

Gathering for a course at the Yellowstone Institute, Lamar Ranger Station.   MICHAEL SAMPLE

Trail riding southwest of Canyon Village. MICHAEL SAMPLE

An experienced horseman on the crew at
Roosevelt Lodge. MICHAEL SAMPLE

66 *I almost wished I could spend the
remainder of my days in a place like this
where happiness and contentment seemed
to reign in wild romantic splendor.* 99

Osborne Russell, 1830s
quoted in *Roadside History of Yellowstone National Park*

Gibbon Falls. JEFF FOOTT

66 *I never understood what Wordsworth meant by "hearing the mighty waters roll" until I stood beside the Gibbon and lost myself in the fullness and variety of its music.* 99

Former park ranger Donald C. Stewart
My Yellowstone Years

A Clark's nutcracker, named after William Clark of the Lewis and Clark Expedition. TOM MURPHY

Dancing water between the ledges and grassy banks of the Gibbon River. JOHN REDDY

The dramatic white flats and humps of Norris Geyser Basin. BUDDY MAYS

" We walked chattering to the uplands of Hell. They call it the Norris Geyser Basin on Earth. . . where green-gray, black-yellow, and pink pools roared, shouted, bubbled, or hissed as their wicked fancies prompted. . . . How was I to tell when the raving blast of steam would find its vent insufficient and blow the whole affair into Nirvana? "

Rudyard Kipling
quoted in *Roadside History of Yellowstone National Park*

Echinus Geyser works its way up to a froth. MICHAEL SAMPLE

A mesmerizing blue-green pool in Norris Geyser Basin.   GEORGE WUERTHNER

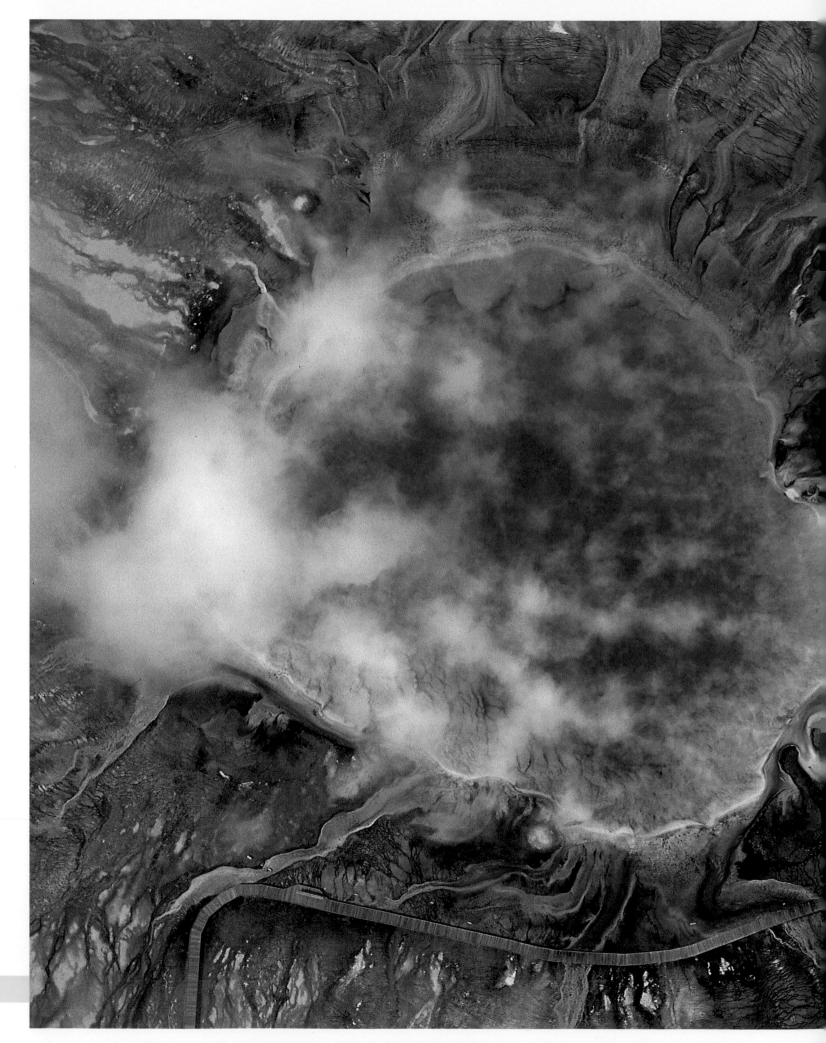

An aerial view of the sunburst made by Midway Basin's Grand Prismatic Spring. MICHAEL SAMPLE

66 *This terrace, to be seen in all its transcendent, golden glory, must be seen between the hours of noon and 2 p.m. Before noon, standing with your back to the [spring] and looking eastward, the reflected light from the golden floor at your feet is so dazzling that the eye cannot endure it.* 99

G. L. Henderson
quoted in *Yellowstone Place Names*

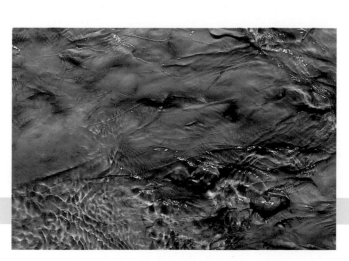

Bacterial growth colors the spring's runoff.
MICHAEL SAMPLE

Park geologist Rick Hutchinson and *National Geographic's* Boyd Mattson use a heat-treated boat called the Little Dipper to sample the park's thermal features. JEFF AND ALEXA HENRY

Beauty Pool, Upper Geyser Basin.   MICHAEL SAMPLE

Artists' Paintpots, mud springs dappled with the colors of a painter's palette.
MICHAEL SAMPLE

The gilded Lower Falls of the Yellowstone at sunrise. MICHAEL SAMPLE

" *Prodigal nature has here outdone herself. As this mighty play of waters plunges amid the rocks, the dense clouds of mist and spray produced by the whirling mass. . . produces a rainbow not only richer in color, but grander and clearer than we had ever seen before. The mountains and valley caught and emphasized the golden rays which were flooding the scene.*

Truly it has been said that the grand in nature more than in art demands homage. "

Lispenard Rutgers
On and Off the Saddle

Climbing from the canyon's depths via Uncle Tom's Trail. JEFF AND ALEXA HENRY

75

An eagle's-eye view of the Grand Canyon and its pinnacles. MICHAEL SAMPLE

❝ The whole gorge flames. . . . The underlying color is the clearest yellow; this flushes onward into orange. Down at the base the deepest mosses unroll their draperies of the most vivid green; browns, sweet and soft, do their blending; white rocks stand spectral; turrets of rock shoot up as crimson as though they were drenched through with blood. It is a wilderness of color. ❞

Wayland Hoyt
quoted in *Marvels of the New West*

Surrounded by a heavy morning fog, trees cling to chutes of soft ash tuff in the Grand Canyon of the Yellowstone.
MICHAEL SAMPLE

Sunset warms the shore of Yellowstone Lake near Solution Creek. GEORGE WUERTHNER

A rainstorm ends with a prism of light on one of the lake's marshy bays. MICHAEL SAMPLE

Storm Point, a peninsula that is often lashed by storms moving northeast across the lake. MICHAEL SAMPLE

❝ Nestled among the forest-crowned hills which bounded our vision, lay this inland sea, its crystal waves dancing and sparkling in the sunlight as if laughing with joy for their wild freedom.❞

David Folsom, 1869
quoted in *Valley of the Upper Yellowstone*

The lush Hayden Valley, excellent feeding grounds for bison and grizzly bears.   MICHAEL SAMPLE

" Even if I were to never set foot in this land again I'd rest easier knowing that these animals were here . . . I am clearly a different person during my exchanges with the creatures of the wilds. And I sense whatever it is that rises to consciousness during those times, is something that's been hidden in the shadows for much too long. "

Gary Ferguson
Walking Down the Wild

A mother bison and her tawny calf.   MICHAEL SAMPLE

A bald eagle preens its tail. JEFF FOOTT

An Alberta wolf crated for transport to Yellowstone.   JEFF AND ALEXA HENRY

66 *Why have I worked so long on behalf of a species for which I profess no special fondness? My romance is with Yellowstone Park's natural system as a whole. I'm captivated by the intricate interplay of wolves; elk; aspen; beetles; ravens; fire; weather; and people, the aspect of the equation all too often overlooked. All these parts—plus thousands we've yet to comprehend—working together in a random yet reciprocal way create the essence of Yellowstone Park: wildness. The circular trail of the wolf leads us there.* 99

Hank Fischer
Wolf Wars

Ready for reintroduction, a male gray wolf awaits freedom. JEFF AND ALEXA HENRY

Wolves being released into holding pens in the Lamar Valley. JEFF AND ALEXA HENRY

The Crystal Creek wolf pack approaching a wary herd of elk and ignoring a herd of bison.   RICK MCINTYRE

66 *More than any other events—more than the occasional soulful howl loosed in the dark of night, more than yearlings wrestling one another and playing king of the mountain on remnant patches of snow—these first encounters between wolves, their prey, and other predators are what burns into my memory. They're the sights that steal breath, that make the sun stop in the sky. On one level it's the first spin of a fresh, fascinating wheel of animal behavior; on the other it has the spark of something ancient, of relationships thousands of years old, fanned back to flame before our eyes.* 99

Wolves on the run.   DENVER BRYAN

Gary Ferguson
Walking Down the Wild

The contoured hills of Crystal Creek, one wolf pack's homeland in the upper Lamar.   MICHAEL SAMPLE

The park's newest activity: wolf watching.   MICHAEL SAMPLE

A bugling bull elk sings the park's traditional autumn song. ERWIN AND PEGGY BAUER

The peak of fall color along the Gardner River. MICHAEL SAMPLE

Master of the Yellowstone wilderness, a grizzly bear during a midday ramble. DONALD M. JONES

❝ As we walk in such beauty we travel back in time . . . . This—come down to the creekside—is how it smelled ten thousand years ago. There—on the ridge—that elk is exactly like the one our forebears saw for a hundred thousand years. They too feared the grizzly bear and laughed at the antics of her cubs. They heard the same wolves howling that we hear tonight, under this same moon. . . .Can we say that Yellowstone is a sacred place? I am uncomfortable with the term, but I know that many people do consider it to be. ❞

Thomas McNamee
The Return of the Wolf to Yellowstone

Stone columns and evergreens stretching up to the light above Tower Fall. MICHAEL SAMPLE

" Nothing can be more chastely beautiful than this lovely cascade, hidden away in the dim light of overshadowing rocks and woods, its very voice hushed to a low murmur unheard at the distance of a few hundred yards. Thousands might pass by within half a mile and not dream of its existence, but once seen, it passes to the list of most pleasant memories. "

Lieutenant Gustavus C. Doane, 1870
quoted in *Yellowstone National Park: Its Exploration and Establishment*

Tower Fall. MICHAEL SAMPLE

Castle Geyser in its full throes.   MICHAEL SAMPLE

66 Our attention was at once attracted by water and steam escaping, or being thrown up from an opening. . . .We could not contain our enthusiasm: with one accord we all took off our hats and yelled with all our might. 99

Charles W. Cook, in notes made during
the Cook-Folsom Expedition of 1870,
quoted in *Yellowstone Explorers Guide*

On a winter morning, Old Faithful shows its classic column and flag. JEFF AND ALEXA HENRY

The historic lodge complex at Old Faithful, offering front-row seats at the geyser's regular shows.   JEFF FOOTT

" Geology provides few rousing hymns. . . . But in Yellowstone we view the planet in its most volatile state, where earthquakes occur daily, and rock is continuously remade and recycled.

In this otherworldly place—where spectacular geysers, lakes, and canyons were the primary justification for designating the world's first national park—it is geology, the mundane realm of rocks, that distinguishes Yellowstone. "

David Cowan
The Yellowstone GeoEcosystem

Ranger Carolyn Evans explaining geyser mechanics to a group of young visitors.

Many-gabled Old Faithful Inn, a top destination on the park's Grand Loop. FRED PFLUGHOFT

> *I built it in keeping with the place where it stands. Nobody could improve upon that. To be at discord with the landscape would be almost a crime. To try to improve upon it, would be an impertinence.*

Old Faithful Inn architect Robert C. Reamer
quoted in *"A Miracle in Hotel Building"*

Peeled logs and river rock fireplace in the Old Faithful Inn's impressive lobby. DAVID M. MORRIS

Visitors get an unexpected shower at Beehive Geyser in the Upper Geyser Basin.   JEFF AND ALEXA HENRY

Rainbow Pool in Black Sand Basin.   MICHAEL SAMPLE

Luminous Morning Glory Pool in the Upper Geyser Basin.   JEFF FOOTT

    At twelve o'clock A.M., August 30th, we arrived in the Upper Geyser Basin of Firehole River, which is the centre of attraction in the National Park, and the grand geyser-region of the world, and where in future years, not far hence, either, the philosophers and tourists, and the lovers of the sublime and the wonderland in Nature, will gather from all countries and climes to make investigation, to behold and wonder, and even worship at Nature's shrine.

Edwin J. Stanley
Rambles in Wonderland, 1878

Watching bison from a safe distance along the Madison River. GEORGE WUERTHNER

❝ *Find a promontory at dawn or dusk, and spread before you will be a landscape of Edenic beauty, the great herds moving slowly along the broad valley floor, the scattered groves of aspen, cottonwood, and spruce more perfectly placed than civilization's greatest gardeners could ever have done, the silence more awesome than the most terrible thunder.* ❞

Thomas McNamee
The Return of the Wolf to Yellowstone

Stunning vistas along the switchbacking East Entrance Road.   MICHAEL SAMPLE

A young black bear with an altitudinal advantage. DENVER BRYAN

A lush opening along Middle Creek near the park's East Entrance.   MICHAEL SAMPLE

Gray jay, also known as "camp robber."   MICHAEL SAMPLE

The Northern Rocky Mountain summer is in full swing. . . . The earth feels like it is pausing, as if it were unhooking the tether on all the life it has nurtured during the warm, sweet days of early summer. There is a kind of magic in the mountains now. And one of the finest, most bewitching illusions it casts is to make you think that it will never end.

Gary Ferguson
Walking Down the Wild

An aspen meadow near the Gardner River opens to views of Electric Peak.   GEORGE WUERTHNER

A bright-eyed chipmunk nibbles its lunch on a weathered log.   MICHAEL SAMPLE

103

A moose in familiar habitat. MICHAEL SAMPLE

The shallow course of Bacon Rind Creek. MICHAEL SAMPLE

Clustering royal blue butterflies.   TOM MURPHY

A muted brown grasshopper hides in a clump of
pearly everlasting.   MICHAEL SAMPLE

A ladybug on native blue-pod lupine.
MICHAEL SAMPLE

Elk dot the greening flanks of Mount Washburn. MICHAEL SAMPLE

" To stand in a shower of sunlight at the feet of these great peaks is to feel like you've made it to the cutting edge of creation. For just a split second my mind stops analyzing, stops comparing what I see to anything I've ever known before. This is all new. Every bit of it. And beneath the quiet, rugged veneer there seems to be the faintest thrum of life erupting—of life being, in Nietzche's words, a great wheel rolling out of its own center. "

Gary Ferguson
Walking Down the Wild

A spotted elk calf and its mother.   CAROL POLICH

107

Evening rays illuminate Upper Soda Butte Creek and The Thunderer mountain.   GEORGE WUERTHNER

A pronghorn buck strolls along its grassland range.   MICHAEL SAMPLE

A rush-lined pond beneath Electric Peak mirrors the golden country. JOHN REDDY

Hiking on a summer snowfield deep in Yellowstone's backcountry. JEFF AND ALEXA HENRY

" *The park endures as one of the most culturally and historically significant places in America. It's to the United States what the Great Barrier Reef is to Australia, the Pyramids are to Egypt, the Galapagos Islands are to Ecuador. It helps define who we are as a nation and what we believe in.* "

Hank Fischer
Wolf Wars

Lichens and snow coat the craggy outcroppings near the Lamar River. MICHAEL SAMPLE

111

On the margin between winter and spring, marsh marigolds and blades of grass
defy the results of a cold night. MICHAEL SAMPLE

Ducks paddle past hoarfrost on a chilly morning. CAROL POLICH

66 *Sunlight dapples the snow-shrouded landscape, glaring through hastily moving clouds and casting shifting, mottled patterns on rolling hills and forest valleys. At its most brilliant, the sun, cutting sharply through clean, crisp air makes the snow glitter as if encrusted with thousands of sparkling diamonds.* 99

Jim Robbins
Last Refuge

Frosted larkspur. MICHAEL SAMPLE

A dusting of snow sparkles like white diamonds amid burned pines. TOM MURPHY

Grizzly sow keeping a watchful eye on her rambunctious cubs.   GLENN VAN NIMWEGEN

Imprinted signs of passage: large and small grizzly tracks in the mud.
MICHAEL SAMPLE

A grizzly bear at dinner on a winterkill. MICHAEL SAMPLE

" A figure of power, majesty, and freedom, the grizzly rules supreme among the native fauna, fearing only man and larger bears. He is noble, defiant, vigorous, mysterious, enduring, courageous, long-lived, mobile, brawny, intelligent, cautious, agile, curious, solitary, fun-loving, and individualistic—traits often admired by man. With his superior physical and mental qualities, the grizzly undoubtedly deserves the title, king of the American wilderness. "

Bill Schneider
Where the Grizzly Walks

The fish-filled Yellowstone River near Mud Volcano.   JEFF AND ALEXA HENRY

66 This is classic nip and tuck country, a topography with the lilt and roll of heavy seas, the main memory bead on the rosary I use to invoke the magic of Yellowstone whenever I'm long away. 99

Gary Ferguson
The Yellowstone Wolves: The First Year

A mostly quiet fish eater, the white pelican.   MICHAEL SAMPLE

An oxbow bend on ancient Pelican Creek. MICHAEL SAMPLE

they made it possible

Yellowstone on My Mind would have been impossible to produce without the keen eyes and technical skills of eighteen professional photographers. These women and men submitted their finest images, and the results show in this stunning collection of photos. What does not show is the work it took to get these images—the early mornings to capture the sunrise, the long climbs through rugged terrain, the endless hours of waiting for the perfect light, the hundreds of shots that didn't turn out quite right, and the high level of technical skill that was acquired through years of experience and study. To all the photographers who contributed to *Yellowstone on My Mind,* we say thanks. We appreciate their art and their hard work.

The Globe Pequot Press

Photographers in *Yellowstone on My Mind*

Denver Bryan

Alan Chapman

Jeff Foott

Chuck Haney

Jeff and Alexa Henry

Don Jones

Buddy Mays/Travel Stock

Rick McIntyre

David M. Morris

Tom Murphy

Carl Oksanen

Fred Pflughoft

Carol Polich

John Reddy

Michael Sample

Glenn Van Nimwegen

George Wuerthner

Library of Congress Number: 98-92652

ISBN 1-56044-380-4

Manufactured in Korea
First Edition/Fourth Printing

www.globe-pequot.com

Title page:
At Yellowstone's North Entrance, Roosevelt Arch is the gateway to nature's wonderland. MICHAEL SAMPLE

End papers:
Cow moose along the Yellowstone River. MICHAEL SAMPLE

acknowledgments

The publisher gratefully acknowledges the following sources:

Pages 1, 14, 40, and 97 from *Rambles in Wonderland; or, A Trip Through the Great Yellowstone National Park*, by Edwin J. Stanley. © 1878 by E. J. Stanley; Publishing House of the Methodist Episcopal Church, South.

Page 3 from *Mountain Time* by Paul Schullery. © 1984 by Paul Schullery; Nick Lyons Books/Shocken Books.

Pages 6 and 47 quoted in "Roughing it up the Yellowstone to Wonderland: The Nelson Miles/Colgate Hoyt Party in Yellowstone National Park, September 1878," by James S. Brust and Lee H. Whittlesey. Published in *Montana, The Magazine of Western History*, Spring 1996.

Pages 9 and 53 from "A Smoke-Scented Diary," by Carol A. Shively. Published in *Natural History* magazine, August 1989.

Pages 11, 21, 33, and 112 from *Last Refuge: The Environmental Showdown in Yellowstone and the American West*, by Jim Robbins. © 1993 by Jim Robbins; William Morrow & Co., Inc.

Pages 18 and 71 quoted in *Yellowstone Place Names* by Lee H. Whittlesey. © 1988 by the Montana Historical Society Press.

Pages 28, 34, 61, 62, 80, 101, and 107 from *Walking Down the Wild: A Journey Through the Yellowstone Rockies*. © 1995 by Gary Ferguson; HarperCollins West.

Page 37 from *The Grizzly Bear* by Thomas McNamee. © 1982, 1984 by Thomas McNamee; Alfred A. Knopf.

Pages 42, 65, and 68 quoted in *Roadside History of Yellowstone Park* by Winfred Blevins. © 1989 by Mountain Press Publishing Co.

Page 45 from *The Yellowstone National Park, Historical and Descriptive* by Hiram Martin Chittenden. © 1895, 1911 by Hiram Martin Chittenden; The Robert Clarke Co.

Page 49 from *The Calumet of the Coteau* by P. W. Norris. © 1883 by P. W. Norris; J. B. Lippincott & Co.

Page 66 from *My Yellowstone Years* by Donald C. Stewart. © 1989 by Donald C. Stewart; Wilderness Adventure Books.

Page 75 from *On and Off the Saddle: Characteristic Sights and Scenes from the Great Northwest to the Antilles* by Lispenard Rutgers. © 1894 by G. P. Putnam's Sons/The Knickerbocker Press.

Pages 76 and 120 from *Marvels of the New West* by William M. Thayer. © 1887 by William M. Thayer; The Henry Bill Publishing Co.

Page 79 from *Valley of the Upper Yellowstone* by Aubrey Haines. © 1965 by Aubrey Haines; University of Oklahoma Press.

Pages 82 and 110 from *Wolf Wars: The Remarkable Inside Story of the Restoration of Wolves to Yellowstone* by Hank Fischer. © 1995 by Falcon Publishing.

Pages 84 and 116 from *The Yellowstone Wolves: The First Year* by Gary Ferguson. © 1996 by Falcon Publishing.

Pages 87 and 98 from *Return of the Wolf to Yellowstone* by Thomas McNamee. ©1997 by Henry Holt and Co., Inc.

Page 88 quoted in *Yellowstone National Park: Its Exploration and Establishment* by Aubrey L. Haines. © 1974 by U.S. Department of the Interior, National Park Service.

Page 90 quoted in *Yellowstone Explorers Guide* by Carl Schreier. © 1983 by Carl Schreier; Homestead Publishing.

Page 92 from "The Yellowstone GeoEcosystem," by David Cowan. Published in the *Greater Yellowstone Report*, Summer 1997.

Page 94 quoted in "A Miracle in Hotel Building" by J. H. Raftery. © 1913. Brochure published by the Yellowstone Park Hotel Co.

Page 115 from *Where the Grizzly Walks* by Bill Schneider. © 1977 by Mountain Press Publishing Co.